I0020982

THE LIMITED EDITION GUIDE TO MASTERING GEMINI AI

BECOME AN EARLY ADOPTER AND SEIZE THE COMPETITIVE EDGE

WRITTEN BY EVAN WALTERS

Chapter	Subtitles
Chapter 1: Welcome to the Future of AI	1.1 What is Gemini AI and Why Should You Care?
	1.2 Unveiling the Potential: A Glimpse into What Gemini AI Can Do
	1.3 Early Adopter Advantage: Why Being First Matters
Chapter 2: Getting Started with Gemini AI	2.1 Setting Up Your Account: A Step-by-Step Guide
	2.2 Navigating the Interface: Mastering the Dashboard and Tools
	2.3 Essential Settings: Fine-Tuning Gemini AI for Your Workflow
Chapter 3: Unleashing Your Inner Powerhouse: Core Features of Gemini AI	3.1 The Power of Language: Text Generation, Translation, and Summarization

Preface: Welcome to the Future with Gemini AI

Greetings, innovators and fellow travelers on the path of progress! Are you ready to **unlock your potential** and **transform the way you work, learn, and create**? Welcome to the exciting world of Gemini AI!

This book is your **comprehensive guide** to understanding and leveraging the remarkable capabilities of Gemini AI. Within these pages, you'll discover **practical strategies** to **streamline workflows, boost creativity, optimize marketing and sales efforts, and fuel innovation** across various aspects of your personal and professional life.

Whether you're a seasoned professional or an eager newcomer to the world of AI, this book caters to you. We'll delve into **cutting-edge advancements** in AI technology, explore **real-world applications** of Gemini AI, and equip you with the knowledge to **become a powerful user and collaborator**.

Here's a glimpse of what awaits you:

- **Actionable insights** on how to automate repetitive tasks, generate creative content, analyze data to gain valuable insights, and develop innovative products and services.
- **Step-by-step instructions** to leverage Gemini AI for marketing campaigns, sales prospecting, data analysis, and brainstorming sessions.
- **Exploration of the ethical considerations surrounding AI development** and guidance on **using Gemini AI responsibly for positive change.**

- **A glimpse into the future of AI** and how Gemini AI might **continue to shape the world in the years to come.**

This book is more than just a user manual; it's an **invitation to a journey of exploration and discovery.** As you partner with Gemini AI, prepare to **unlock hidden possibilities, enhance your productivity, and push the boundaries of what's achievable.**

So, buckle up and get ready to experience the transformative power of AI! With Gemini AI as your guide, the future is bright and full of unprecedented possibilities.

Chapter 1: Welcome to the Future of AI

Welcome! This chapter serves as your launchpad into the exciting world of Gemini AI. We'll begin by exploring the concept of Artificial Intelligence (AI) and then delve into the innovative capabilities of Gemini AI, a powerful tool designed to revolutionize workflows across various fields.

1.1 What is Gemini AI and Why Should You Care?

Welcome to the world of Gemini AI! In this section, we'll break down what Gemini AI is and why it can be a valuable asset in your toolbox.

Introducing Gemini AI:

Gemini AI is a cutting-edge tool powered by Artificial Intelligence (AI). AI refers to the ability of machines to simulate human cognitive functions, such as learning, reasoning, and problem-solving. In simpler terms, AI allows computers to process information, identify patterns, and even make decisions in a way that mimics human intelligence.

What Makes Gemini AI Special?

Specifically, Gemini AI is designed to excel in tasks involving language processing and creative generation. Think of it as a powerful language assistant on steroids. Here are some key capabilities:

- **Understanding Your Needs:** Gemini AI can analyze your requests and respond accordingly. Imagine having a tool that can grasp your intent and generate text that aligns with your goals.

- **Generating Text:** Need help crafting compelling content, translating languages, or brainstorming ideas? Gemini AI can assist you in generating high-quality text formats to meet your specific needs.

Why Should You Care?

Here's why Gemini AI can be a game-changer:

- **Boost Productivity:** Automate repetitive tasks and generate content efficiently, freeing up your time to focus on higher-level projects.

- **Enhance Creativity:** Overcome writer's block or generate fresh ideas with the help of AI-powered suggestions and tools.
- **Stay Ahead of the Curve:** AI is rapidly transforming various industries. By familiarizing yourself with Gemini AI, you'll be well-equipped to leverage this powerful technology.

Whether you're a beginner or an experienced developer, Gemini AI offers a user-friendly platform that can significantly enhance your workflow. As we move forward, we'll delve deeper into the functionalities of Gemini AI, empowering you to unlock its full potential.

1.2 Unveiling the Potential: A Glimpse into What Gemini AI Can Do

Now that you understand the core concept of Gemini AI, let's explore its exciting capabilities in more detail. Imagine having a powerful language assistant by your side, ready to tackle various tasks and unleash your creative potential. Here's how Gemini AI can transform your workflow:

- **Content Creation Powerhouse:**

- **Effortless Writing:** Struggling to write engaging blog posts, social media captions, or even marketing copy? Gemini AI can generate high-quality drafts based on your prompts and specifications. Need help crafting a captivating product description? Gemini AI can provide suggestions and variations to jumpstart your creativity.
- **Say Goodbye to Writer's Block:** Stuck staring at a blank page? Utilize Gemini AI's brainstorming features to generate fresh ideas and overcome writer's block.

- **Research and Analysis Simplified:**
  - **Information Gathering Made Easy:** Researching a new topic can be time-consuming. Gemini AI can help you gather relevant information and summarize complex research papers, saving you valuable time and effort.
  - **Data Analysis on Autopilot:** Need to analyze large amounts of text data? Gemini AI can assist you in identifying key trends and insights, streamlining your research process.

- **Workflow Automation for Efficiency:**
  - **Repetitive Tasks Be Gone:** Tired of spending hours on repetitive tasks like data entry or email drafting? Gemini AI can automate these tasks, freeing you to focus on more strategic initiatives.
  - **Boost Your Productivity:** By automating repetitive tasks and generating content efficiently, Gemini AI empowers you to accomplish more in less time.

These are just a few examples of Gemini AI's vast potential. As you explore the tool further, you'll discover even more ways to leverage its capabilities and transform your workflow. We'll delve deeper into these functionalities in the coming chapters, equipping you to unlock the full potential of Gemini AI.

1.3 Early Adopter Advantage: Why Being First Matters

In today's rapidly evolving technological landscape, being an early adopter of innovative tools like Gemini AI offers significant advantages. Here's why getting started with Gemini AI now can be a strategic move:

- **Gain a Competitive Edge:** By familiarizing yourself with Gemini AI early on, you develop a valuable skillset. This positions you as a skilled user with a powerful tool at your disposal. Imagine being able to leverage AI-powered content creation and workflow automation to outperform competitors who haven't yet embraced this technology.

- **Shape the Future of AI:** Early adopters play a crucial role in shaping the future of platforms like Gemini AI. Your feedback and suggestions directly influence the tool's development. As you explore and utilize Gemini AI, you'll have the opportunity to provide valuable insights that can contribute to its continuous improvement and ensure it remains user-friendly and relevant for everyone.

- **Unlock Hidden Potential:** New technologies often have a learning curve. By starting early, you have the opportunity to explore all the functionalities of Gemini AI at your own pace. This allows you to discover hidden potential and uncover unique ways to integrate the tool into your workflow, maximizing its benefits for your specific needs.

The Takeaway: Don't miss out on being a pioneer! By taking the initiative to learn and utilize Gemini AI now, you gain a valuable head start, position yourself for success in the AI-driven future, and contribute to shaping a powerful tool that benefits everyone.

Chapter 2: Getting Started with Gemini AI

Welcome to your gateway into the world of Gemini AI! This chapter serves as your launchpad, guiding you through the essential steps to set up your account, navigate the interface, and customize your experience.

2.1 Setting Up Your Account: A Step-by-Step Guide

Congratulations on taking the first step towards unleashing the power of Gemini AI! This section will guide you effortlessly through the account setup process.

Here's what you'll need:

- A computer or mobile device with internet access
- A valid email address (or an existing Google account)

Ready? Let's begin!

1. **Launchpad Awaits:** Open your preferred web browser and navigate to the official Gemini AI website. **[Due to policy restrictions, we cannot provide the link here, but you can find it with a quick web search].**

2. **Sign Up for Exploration:**
Once you arrive at the Gemini
AI website, locate the clear and
prominent "Sign Up" button.
Click on it to initiate the account
creation process.

3. **Choose Your Path:** You'll
typically be presented with two
options for creating your
account:

   - **Email Address:** Enter a
valid email address and
create a unique password.
This email address will serve
as your login credential for
Gemini AI.

- **Google Account:** If you have an existing Google account, you can conveniently use it to sign up for Gemini AI. This option streamlines the process by leveraging your existing Google login information.

4. **Follow the Trail:** Regardless of the signup method you choose, you'll be guided through a series of on-screen instructions. These instructions are straightforward and easy to follow. Be sure to provide any required information accurately.

5. **Welcome Aboard!:** Once you've completed the signup process, you'll be greeted with a warm welcome message from Gemini AI. Congratulations, you're now a registered user!

Optional Step: Take the Tour (or Dive Right In!)

- Gemini AI often provides an optional introductory tutorial after successful signup. This tutorial offers a brief overview of the interface and core functionalities.
- If you're eager to start exploring, you can skip the tutorial and proceed directly to the Gemini AI interface.

Remember: You can always access the tutorial later if you feel the need for a refresher.

By following these simple steps, you'll have your Gemini AI account up and running in no time. Get ready to embark on a journey of enhanced productivity and limitless creative potential!

2.2 Navigating the Interface: Mastering the Dashboard and Tools

Welcome to your Gemini AI command center! This chapter equips you with the knowledge to navigate the user-friendly interface and unlock the full potential of its various tools.

Demystifying the Dashboard: Your Central Hub

Imagine the Gemini AI dashboard as your mission control center. Here's what you'll find:

- **At-a-Glance Overview**: Gain quick insights into your recent activities, such as the number of tasks completed or the types of tools you've used most frequently.
- **Quick Access Points**: Easily locate commonly used features or access ongoing projects through convenient shortcuts and buttons. This section helps you jump right into the tasks at hand.

- **Helpful Resources:** Gemini AI often provides helpful tips, tutorials, and guides directly within the dashboard. These resources can assist you in mastering specific functionalities or exploring new features.

Exploring the Feature Menu: Your Toolbox of Options

Think of the feature menu as your toolbox, neatly organized with all the tools Gemini AI has to offer. Here's a breakdown of its typical structure:

- **Categorized Functionality:** Features are typically grouped into logical categories based on their purpose. For example, you might see categories like "Content Creation," "Research Assistance," or "Workflow Automation."
- **Clear Labels:** Each feature has a clear and concise title that reflects its function. This allows you to easily identify the tool that best suits your needs.
- **Intuitive Navigation:** The interface is designed for ease of use. You can navigate through the menu using clear labels and simple dropdown menus to locate the desired tool.

Understanding the Workspace: Where the Magic Happens!

Once you've selected a specific feature from the menu, you'll be directed to the dedicated workspace. This is where the real action takes place! Here's what you can expect:

- **Contextual Interface:** The workspace layout and options will dynamically adjust based on the chosen feature. For instance, the workspace for content creation might include prompts for topic selection and style preferences, while the research assistance workspace might offer options for keyword input and source filtering.
- **Interactive Elements:** The workspace provides interactive elements like text fields, dropdown menus, and buttons to allow you to interact with Gemini AI and provide the necessary information or instructions.

- **Output Delivery:** Depending on the chosen feature, the workspace will display Gemini AI's generated text, summarized information, or completed tasks within the designated output area.

Pro Tip: Always pay attention to the helpful tooltips and on-screen instructions that often appear within the workspace. These can provide valuable guidance for using specific features most effectively.

Mastering the Interface: A Seamless Experience

By familiarizing yourself with the core elements of the Gemini AI interface – the dashboard, feature menu, and workspace – you'll be well-equipped to navigate seamlessly and unlock the power of its diverse tools. In the following chapters, we'll delve deeper into each feature, providing detailed instructions and practical examples to help you master specific functionalities and optimize your workflow.

2.3 Essential Settings: Fine-Tuning Gemini AI for Your Workflow

Welcome to the customization corner! This section empowers you to personalize your Gemini AI experience by adjusting key settings to optimize its functionality for your specific needs.

Tailoring the Output: Preferences for Flawless Results

Gemini AI offers various settings to ensure the output aligns perfectly with your requirements. Here are some crucial settings to explore:

- **Output Language:** Select your preferred language for receiving results from Gemini AI. This allows you to utilize the tool seamlessly, regardless of your native language.

- **Content Style:** Do you need formal writing for a business report or a casual tone for a social media post? Adjust the content style setting to match your project's specific needs. Options might include "Formal," "Informal," "Creative," or even "Technical."
- **Content Length:** Depending on the task, you might prefer concise summaries or more elaborate content generation. Utilize the content length setting to control the output size, ranging from short snippets to comprehensive drafts.

- **Specificity Options:** For certain features, you might be able to adjust the level of specificity in the generated text. This allows you to fine-tune the results to match your desired level of detail and focus.

Privacy and Security: Maintaining Control Over Your Data

Peace of mind is crucial. Here are some settings related to privacy and security:

- **Data Usage Preferences:** Review and adjust your data usage preferences to control how your information is used within the platform.

- **Account Security:** Ensure the security of your account by enabling two-factor authentication or setting up strong password protocols.

Exploring Advanced Settings (Optional):

Gemini AI might offer additional settings for experienced users to further customize their experience. These settings could involve:

- **Advanced Output Formatting:** Control the formatting of the generated text, such as line spacing, paragraph breaks, or bullet points.

- **Integration Options:** Connect your Gemini AI account with other tools you frequently use, streamlining your workflow further.

Remember: Don't hesitate to experiment with different settings to discover what works best for you. As you explore Gemini AI's functionalities, revisit the settings section regularly to fine-tune your experience and maximize the tool's effectiveness for your specific needs.

By taking advantage of these customization options, you'll transform Gemini AI from a powerful tool into a personalized assistant, perfectly tailored to enhance your workflow and unleash your creative potential.

Chapter 3: Unleashing Your Inner Powerhouse: Core Features of Gemini AI

Congratulations! You've mastered the basics of navigating Gemini AI. Now, it's time to delve into the heart of the matter – its core features. In this chapter, we'll explore the functionalities that empower you to become a productivity powerhouse and unleash your creative potential.

Unveiling the Powerhouse: A Look at Key Features

Gemini AI boasts a diverse range of features designed to streamline your workflow and enhance your creativity across various tasks. Here's a glimpse into some of the most powerful tools at your disposal:

- **The Language Maestro: Text Generation and Manipulation**

- Craft compelling content effortlessly: Generate high-quality blog posts, social media captions, or even marketing copy based on your prompts and specifications. Overcome writer's block and jumpstart your creative process with a variety of text generation options.
- Transform existing content: Rephrase sentences, summarize lengthy passages, or even translate languages with remarkable accuracy, saving you valuable time and effort.

- **Research Assistant on Autopilot**
  - Become an information ninja: Effortlessly gather relevant information and summarize complex research papers or articles. Gemini AI can analyze vast amounts of data, identify key trends, and present you with concise and insightful summaries.
  - Fact-check with ease: Ensure the accuracy of your information by utilizing Gemini AI's fact-checking capabilities.
- **Workflow Automation for Efficiency**

- Say goodbye to repetitive tasks: Automate repetitive tasks that drain your time and energy. Gemini AI can handle data entry, email drafting, and other tedious tasks, allowing you to focus on higher-level projects and strategic initiatives.
- Build custom workflows: For complex tasks involving multiple steps, Gemini AI allows you to create custom workflows, streamlining your processes and boosting your overall productivity.

Remember: This is just a taste of the possibilities. As you delve deeper into each feature in the following chapters, you'll discover even more ways to leverage Gemini AI's capabilities and transform your workflow.

The Power is in Your Hands:

By mastering the core features of Gemini AI, you unlock a treasure trove of benefits:

- **Enhanced Productivity:** Automate tasks, generate content efficiently, and streamline your workflow, freeing up valuable time and energy for other endeavors.

- **Boosted Creativity:** Overcome writer's block, generate fresh ideas, and explore new creative avenues with the help of AI-powered tools.
- **Improved Accuracy:** Ensure the accuracy of your information with fact-checking features and access to reliable sources through research assistance.
- **Competitive Edge:** Position yourself as a skilled user with a powerful tool at your disposal, gaining an edge in today's AI-driven landscape.

Get ready to unleash your inner powerhouse! The following chapters will equip you with the knowledge and skills to master each core feature of Gemini AI and unlock its full potential.

3.1 The Power of Language: Text Generation, Translation, and Summarization

Dive deeper into the world of words with Gemini AI's language processing features! This section explores the functionalities that empower you to become a master of communication and content creation.

1. Text Generation: Effortless Content Creation at Your Fingertips

- **Content Creation Powerhouse:**
  - **Say goodbye to blank slates:** Struggling to write engaging blog posts, social media captions, or product descriptions? Gemini AI can generate high-quality drafts based on your input and specifications. Provide a brief description of your topic, target audience, and desired tone, and let Gemini AI craft compelling content to jumpstart your creative process.

- ○ **Beat writer's block:** Staring at a blank page can be daunting. Utilize Gemini AI's brainstorming features to generate fresh ideas, explore different creative angles, and overcome writer's block. Whether you need catchy headlines, captivating introductions, or persuasive arguments, Gemini AI can provide a spark to ignite your writing.
- **Text Manipulation Made Easy:**

- **Rephrase for clarity:** Fine-tune your writing by rephrasing sentences or paragraphs for improved clarity and conciseness. Gemini AI can offer alternative phrasings while preserving the original meaning of your text.
- **Summarize with precision:** Need to condense lengthy articles or research papers into concise summaries? Gemini AI can analyze vast amounts of text and extract key information, saving you time and effort while ensuring you grasp the essential points.

2. Bridging the Gap: Seamless Language Translation

- **Multilingual Communication:** Break down language barriers and communicate with a global audience. Utilize Gemini AI's translation capabilities to translate text between a wide range languages with remarkable accuracy.

- **Context-Aware Translations:** Gemini AI goes beyond simple word-for-word translations. It considers the context of your text to ensure translated content reads naturally and conveys the intended meaning accurately.

3. Mastering Information: Text Summarization

- **Information at a Glance:** Quickly grasp the key points of lengthy documents or research papers with AI-powered summarization. Gemini AI can analyze complex texts and generate concise summaries that highlight the most important information.

- **Enhanced Research Efficiency:** Save valuable time when conducting research by utilizing Gemini AI's summarization features. Efficiently process large amounts of textual data and identify critical insights to inform your research endeavors.

Remember: These are just a few examples of Gemini AI's language processing capabilities. As you explore further, you'll discover even more ways to leverage these tools to streamline your workflow, enhance your communication, and unleash your creative potential.

The following chapters will provide a more in-depth exploration of each functionality, including step-by-step guides and practical examples to help you master these powerful language tools.

3.2 Boosting Creativity: Brainstorming, Content Ideas, and Scriptwriting Assistance

Unleash your inner creative genius with Gemini AI's innovative features designed to spark inspiration and streamline the content creation process.

1. Brainstorming Bonanza: Generate Fresh Ideas and Overcome Blocks

- **Ideation on Autopilot:** Overcome writer's block and generate a multitude of creative ideas with the help of AI-powered brainstorming tools. Simply provide a keyword or a brief description of your topic, and Gemini AI will suggest various creative angles, potential storylines, or unexpected approaches to jumpstart your thinking process.

- **Breakthrough Innovation:** Explore new possibilities and challenge your creative perspective with unexpected ideas generated by Gemini AI. These suggestions can spark new lines of thought and lead you to innovative solutions or unique content concepts.

2. Content Idea Generation: Craft Compelling Content Across Platforms

- **Content Inspiration for All Needs:** Whether you're crafting captivating blog posts, engaging social media captions, or informative website copy, Gemini AI can provide a wealth of content ideas tailored to your specific needs. Describe your target audience and the overall theme, and let Gemini AI generate a list of potential titles, hooks, or content formats to ignite your creative spark.

- **Staying on Trend:** Never miss a beat! Gemini AI can analyze current trends and popular content formats to suggest relevant ideas that resonate with your audience and keep your content fresh and engaging.

3. Scriptwriting Support: From Concept to Completion

- **Storytelling Simplified:** Streamline your scriptwriting process with the assistance of Gemini AI. Develop captivating storylines, craft realistic dialogue, and generate scene descriptions to bring your narrative to life. Provide basic details about your characters and plot, and allow Gemini AI to offer suggestions and variations to enhance your script's flow and emotional impact.

- **Dialogue that Captivates:** Craft natural-sounding dialogue that moves the story forward and reveals your characters' personalities. Gemini AI can assist you in generating realistic conversations that enhance the overall quality of your script.

Remember: These features are designed to empower your creativity, not replace it. Use Gemini AI's suggestions as a springboard to fuel your own ideas and develop unique content that reflects your voice and vision.

The following chapters will delve deeper into each of these functionalities, providing step-by-step instructions and practical examples to illustrate how you can leverage them to maximize your creative potential in various content creation scenarios.

3.3 Optimizing Workflow: Automation, Task Management, and Research Tools

Welcome to the chapter dedicated to transforming your workflow! In this section, we'll explore Gemini AI's functionalities designed to streamline your processes, free up your time, and empower you to accomplish more in less time.

1. Automating Repetitive Tasks: Reclaim Your Time

- **Say Goodbye to Tedium:** Free yourself from the burden of repetitive tasks that drain your time and energy. Gemini AI can automate tasks like data entry, email drafting, and calendar management, allowing you to focus on higher-level projects and strategic initiatives.

- **Customizable Automations:** Design automations that perfectly match your workflow. Specify the triggers and actions for each task, ensuring Gemini AI handles them efficiently and accurately.

2. Task Management Made Easy: Stay Organized and Focused

- **Centralized Hub for Action:** Organize your tasks and projects within Gemini AI's user-friendly interface. Create to-do lists, set deadlines, and track your progress to maintain focus and ensure timely completion of all your tasks.

- **Prioritization Power:** Not all tasks are created equal. Gemini AI can assist you in prioritizing your workload based on urgency and importance, helping you stay on top of critical tasks and deadlines.

3. Research Assistant at Your Fingertips: Effortless Information Gathering

- **Information Powerhouse:** Conduct research with ease and efficiency. Utilize Gemini AI to gather relevant information from various sources, including online articles, academic journals, and databases.

- **AI-Powered Insights:** Go beyond simple data gathering. Gemini AI can analyze the collected information, identify key trends, and generate insightful summaries to inform your research and decision-making processes.

- **Fact-Checking on Autopilot:** Ensure the accuracy of your information by leveraging Gemini AI's fact-checking capabilities. Access reliable sources and verify the credibility of data to maintain the integrity of your research and communication.

Remember: By combining automation, task management, and research assistance features, you can create a streamlined workflow that optimizes your productivity and empowers you to achieve more in less time.

The following chapters will provide a more in-depth exploration of each functionality, including step-by-step guides and practical examples to demonstrate how you can leverage them to transform your workflow and become a productivity powerhouse.

Chapter 4: Deep Dive into Text Generation: Mastering the Art of AI-Powered Writing

Welcome back, aspiring wordsmith! Now that you're familiar with the core functionalities of Gemini AI, let's delve deeper into the exciting world of text generation. This chapter equips you with the knowledge and skills to become an expert user of Gemini AI's writing assistance features.

Unlocking the Potential: A Look at Text Generation Options

Gemini AI's text generation capabilities offer a versatile toolbox for various content creation needs. Here's a breakdown of the primary functionalities you'll explore:

- **Content Creation from Scratch:** Jumpstart your creative process by generating drafts of blog posts, social media content, marketing copy, or even creative text formats like poems or scripts. Provide Gemini AI with essential details like your target audience, desired tone, and a brief topic description.

- **Content Repurposing and Expansion:** Breathe new life into existing content! Rewrite sentences or paragraphs to enhance clarity, summarize lengthy articles, or even expand on existing ideas to generate fresh content variations.
- **Overcoming Writer's Block:** Staring at a blank page is a thing of the past. Utilize brainstorming features to generate creative ideas, explore different writing angles, and break through writer's block.

Taking Control: Tailoring Text Generation to Your Needs

To maximize the effectiveness of text generation, here are key elements you can customize:

- **Content Style:** Specify the desired writing style, ranging from formal and informative to casual and conversational.
- **Content Length:** Control the length of the generated text, from short snippets to comprehensive drafts, depending on your specific needs.

- **Specificity:** Adjust the level of detail in the generated content. Provide more keywords or specific instructions for a highly focused output, or allow for broader creativity with less specific prompts.

Crafting the Perfect Prompt: The Secret Ingredient

The quality of your prompts significantly influences the outcome of text generation. Here are some tips for crafting effective prompts:

- **Clarity is Key:** Provide clear and concise instructions that accurately reflect your desired content.

- **Target Audience Matters:** Specify who you're writing for. Understanding your audience's needs and preferences helps Gemini AI tailor the content accordingly.
- **Keywords and Examples:** Include relevant keywords and provide examples (if applicable) to guide Gemini AI in the right direction.
- **Context is King:** The more context you provide, the better Gemini AI can understand your intent and generate content that aligns with your vision.

Pro Tip: Don't be afraid to experiment! Try different prompts, adjust settings, and see what works best for your specific writing style and content needs.

The Power is in Your Hands: Editing and Refining

Remember, Gemini AI's generated text serves as a starting point. You retain complete control over the final product. Utilize your editing skills to refine the text, ensuring it aligns perfectly with your voice and objectives.

By mastering the text generation features and following these helpful tips, you'll transform Gemini AI into a powerful writing assistant, empowering you to:

- **Boost Productivity:** Generate high-quality content drafts efficiently, freeing up time for other crucial tasks.
- **Overcome Writer's Block:** Break through creative roadblocks and generate fresh ideas to keep your content flowing.
- **Enhance Creativity:** Explore new writing styles and content formats to engage your audience and achieve your goals.

The following sections will provide step-by-step guides and practical examples to illustrate how to leverage text generation for various content creation scenarios. Get ready to unleash your inner writer and craft compelling content with the help of AI!

4.1 From Blank Page to Brilliant Content: Different Text Generation Modes

Welcome to the exciting world of crafting content with Gemini AI! This section dives into the various text generation modes available, empowering you to choose the perfect tool for your specific needs.

Understanding Your Options: A Look at Text Generation Modes

Gemini AI offers a range of text generation modes, each catering to different writing scenarios. Here's a breakdown of the most common functionalities:

- **Blog Post Ideation and Writing:** Struggling to develop captivating blog post topics or jumpstart your writing process? This mode can generate creative blog post titles, outlines, introductions, and even complete drafts based on your chosen topic and target audience.

- **Social Media Magic:** Craft engaging social media captions and posts that resonate with your audience. This mode can generate catchy headlines, attention-grabbing hooks, and creative content formats specifically tailored for various social media platforms.
- **Marketing Copywriting Assistant:** Need persuasive marketing copy or product descriptions? This mode can generate compelling ad copy, email marketing materials, or product descriptions that highlight key features and benefits, driving engagement and sales.

- **Content Repurposing and Expansion:** Breathe new life into existing content! This mode allows you to rewrite sentences for clarity, summarize lengthy articles, or even expand on existing ideas to generate fresh content variations.
- **Creative Text Formats:** Looking to explore beyond traditional writing? This mode offers functionalities for generating creative text formats like poems, code, scripts, musical pieces, and even email replies, depending on your specific needs.

Choosing the Right Mode: Matching Your Needs with Functionality

Selecting the most effective mode is crucial for optimal results. Here are some considerations to guide you:

- **Content Type:** Are you writing a blog post, social media caption, or marketing copy? Choose the mode specifically designed for your content type to ensure relevant outputs.

- **Content Goal:** Do you need help brainstorming ideas, generating drafts, or simply refining existing content? Understanding your objective will help you select the mode that best supports your goals.
- **Desired Tone:** Formal, informal, persuasive, or creative? Specify the desired tone within the chosen mode to ensure the generated text aligns with your overall style and purpose.

Pro Tip: Gemini AI often provides additional options within each mode. For instance, the blog post writing mode might allow you to specify the post length or desired level of formality. Explore these options to further customize the generated content.

The following sections will provide step-by-step instructions and practical examples for each text generation mode, empowering you to craft compelling content across various formats.

4.2 Fine-Tuning Your Results: Prompts, Instructions, and Advanced Customization

Welcome back, wordsmith extraordinaire! Now that you've explored the different text generation modes offered by Gemini AI, this section equips you with the knowledge to fine-tune your prompts and instructions for optimal results. By strategically crafting your input, you'll unlock the full potential of Gemini AI and generate content that perfectly aligns with your vision.

The Power of the Prompt: Crafting Instructions that Guide Gemini AI

The prompt serves as the foundation for your content generation. It outlines the key details that instruct Gemini AI on what to create. Here's how to craft effective prompts:

- **Clarity is King:** Ensure your prompt is clear, concise, and easy to understand. Avoid ambiguity and provide all the necessary information upfront.
- **Target Audience in Mind:** Who are you writing for? Specifying your target audience allows Gemini AI to tailor the content's tone, style, and level of complexity to resonate with your readers.

- **Keywords and Examples:** Include relevant keywords and provide specific examples (if applicable) to guide Gemini AI in the right direction. The more context you provide, the better Gemini AI can understand your intent.
- **Desired Outcome:** Clearly communicate what you want to achieve with the generated content. Are you looking for a comprehensive draft, a creative introduction, or a catchy headline? Specificity is key.

Pro Tip: Read your prompt carefully before submitting it to Gemini AI. Ensure it accurately reflects your desired content and doesn't contain any misleading or irrelevant information.

Taking Control: Advanced Customization Options

In addition to crafting effective prompts, Gemini AI offers advanced customization options to further refine your generated text:

- **Content Style:** Specify the desired writing style, ranging from formal and informative to casual and conversational.

- **Content Length:** Control the length of the generated text, from short snippets to comprehensive drafts, depending on your specific needs.
- **Specificity:** Adjust the level of detail in the generated content. Provide more keywords or specific instructions for a highly focused output, or allow for broader creativity with less specific prompts.

Using Examples to Illustrate Your Vision

- **Show, Don't Just Tell:** Whenever possible, provide examples to illustrate the style, tone, or format you envision for the generated content. This can be particularly helpful for creative text formats like poems or scripts.

Refining Your Craft: The Iterative Process

The first draft generated by Gemini AI might not always be perfect. That's okay! The beauty of AI-powered writing assistance lies in the iterative process. Here's how to refine your results:

- **Review and Edit:** Carefully analyze the generated content and identify areas for improvement.
- **Refine Your Prompt:** Based on the initial output, adjust your prompt to provide more specific instructions or address any inconsistencies.
- **Utilize Feedback Options:** Some Gemini AI features might allow you to provide feedback on the generated content, which can further improve future outputs tailored to your preferences.

Remember: The more you practice crafting prompts and utilizing the customization options, the more comfortable you'll become with fine-tuning your results and generating content that meets your exact requirements.

The following sections will showcase step-by-step examples for various text generation modes, incorporating these advanced customization techniques. Get ready to transform your content creation process and craft high-quality, unique content with the help of Gemini AI!

4.3 Avoiding the Pitfalls: Ensuring Accuracy, Originality, and Avoiding Plagiarism

As with any powerful tool, using Gemini AI for text generation comes with certain considerations. This section equips you with the knowledge to ensure the accuracy, originality, and plagiarism-free nature of your content.

Maintaining Accuracy: Fact-Checking and Verification

While Gemini AI strives to provide factual information, it's crucial to remember it is a machine learning model and may not always have access to the latest updates or nuanced details. Here's how to ensure accuracy:

- **Double-Check Facts:** Don't rely solely on the generated content, especially for factual topics. Conduct your own research and verify the accuracy of information, particularly when dealing with sensitive or critical subjects.

- **Use Reliable Sources:** When possible, instruct Gemini AI to generate content based on credible sources you can verify. This can be particularly helpful for research-driven writing or reports.
- **Stay Updated:** The world is constantly changing, and so is information. Be mindful of the timeliness of the data used by Gemini AI, and consider incorporating recent updates or developments when necessary.

Ensuring Originality: Avoiding Recycled Content

While Gemini AI can be a great tool for paraphrasing and summarizing existing content, it's important to maintain originality in your writing. Here's how to strike a balance:

- **Inject Your Voice and Ideas:** Don't simply copy the generated content. Use it as a springboard to develop your own ideas and express them in your unique voice.

- **Fact-Checking for Originality:** Double-check the generated content for unintentional plagiarism, especially if you're heavily relying on summaries or paraphrased text. Consider using plagiarism checking tools for an extra layer of security.

- **Focus on Uniqueness:** Leverage Gemini AI for tasks that support your creative process, but strive to bring your own unique perspective and insights to the forefront of your writing.

Avoiding Plagiarism: Understanding and Maintaining Ethical Practices

Plagiarism is a serious offense. Here's how to ensure your AI-generated content remains plagiarism-free:

- **Proper Citation:** If you use any excerpts or factual information directly from the generated content, be sure to cite Gemini AI as a source.
- **Transparency is Key:** Disclose that you used AI assistance in your writing process, especially if required by your institution or publication guidelines.
- **Focus on Transformation:** Don't rely solely on copying or paraphrasing from the generated text. Use it as a stepping stone to develop your own original ideas and arguments.

Remember: Ethical and responsible use of AI writing assistants is crucial. By following these best practices, you can leverage the power of Gemini AI to enhance your content creation while maintaining the integrity and originality of your work.

The next section will provide a helpful checklist summarizing the key takeaways from this chapter, empowering you to use Gemini AI for text generation effectively and ethically.

Chapter 5: Content Creation on Autopilot: Streamlining Your Workflow with Gemini AI

Welcome back, productivity champions! Having mastered the art of AI-powered text generation, let's delve into the world of workflow automation and explore how Gemini AI can transform the way you work. This chapter equips you with the knowledge and tools to streamline your processes, free up valuable time, and achieve more in less time.

The Power of Automation: Repetitive Tasks Made Easy

Imagine a world where tedious tasks handle themselves while you focus on higher-level projects. This is the magic of automation! Gemini AI allows you to automate various repetitive tasks that often drain your time and energy. Here are some examples:

- **Data Entry Automation:** Free yourself from the burden of manual data entry. Gemini AI can handle tasks like form completion, data scraping, and list generation based on your predefined rules and instructions.

- **Email Drafting Assistant:** Crafting personalized emails can be time-consuming. Utilize Gemini AI to generate email drafts based on templates or specific parameters, allowing you to personalize them with a quick touch.
- **Calendar Management Made Easy:** Schedule meetings, set reminders, and manage your calendar effortlessly. Integrate Gemini AI with your calendar software to automate scheduling tasks and free up your time for more strategic initiatives.

The Art of Task Management: Staying Organized and Focused

Even the most powerful automation tools require a well-organized system. Here's how to leverage Gemini AI's task management features to stay on top of your workload:

- **Centralized Task Hub:** Consolidate your to-do lists within Gemini AI's user-friendly interface. Create tasks, assign deadlines, and set priorities to maintain a clear overview of your workload.
- **Prioritization Powerhouse:** Not all tasks are created equal. Utilize Gemini AI's prioritization features to focus on critical tasks first and ensure you meet deadlines effectively.

- **Collaboration Made Simple:** Working on projects with a team? Utilize Gemini AI's collaboration features to assign tasks, share documents, and track progress seamlessly within the platform.

Research Assistant at Your Fingertips: Effortless Information Gathering

Research is crucial for many tasks, but it can be time-consuming. Gemini AI can be your research assistant, empowering you to:

- **Information Gathering on Autopilot:** Utilize Gemini AI to gather relevant information from various sources, including online articles, academic journals, and databases. Simply provide keywords or topics, and let Gemini AI compile the data for you.
- **Intelligent Analysis:** Go beyond simple data collection. Gemini AI can analyze the gathered information, identify key trends, and generate insightful summaries to inform your decision-making processes.

- **Fact-Checking on Autopilot:**
Ensure the accuracy of your
information by leveraging
Gemini AI's fact-checking
capabilities. Access reliable
sources and verify the credibility
of data to maintain the integrity
of your research and
communication.

Building Your Automated Workflow: A Step-by-Step Guide

The beauty of automation lies in its
customizability. Here's a general
roadmap to get you started with
building automated workflows in
Gemini AI:

1. **Identify Repetitive Tasks:** Pinpoint the repetitive tasks that consume your valuable time and hinder your productivity.
2. **Break Down the Process:** Analyze each task and break it down into smaller, actionable steps.
3. **Utilize Gemini AI Features:** Match each step of the process with the most relevant Gemini AI feature (e.g., data entry automation, email drafting, calendar management).

4. **Set Triggers and Actions:** Define the triggers that initiate the automation (e.g., receiving a new email) and the actions Gemini AI should perform (e.g., automatically populate a form).
5. **Test and Refine:** Once you've built your workflow, test it thoroughly and make adjustments as needed to ensure it functions smoothly and delivers the desired results.

Remember: Automation is an ongoing process. As your needs evolve, revisit and refine your workflows to maintain their effectiveness and maximize your productivity gains.

The following sections will provide in-depth explorations of each workflow optimization feature, including step-by-step instructions and practical examples to illustrate how to leverage them across various content creation scenarios. Get ready to transform your workflow and become a productivity powerhouse with the help of Gemini AI!

5.1 Blog Posts, Articles, and Social Media Content: Effortless Content Creation

In today's fast-paced digital world, consistent content creation is crucial. This section dives into how Gemini AI can streamline your workflow and empower you to generate high-quality content for blog posts, articles, and social media platforms, saving you time and effort.

From Brainstorming to Publication: A Streamlined Content Creation Process

Let's break down the content creation process and explore how Gemini AI can assist you at each stage:

- **Ideation and Brainstorming:** Stuck for blog post topics or social media captions? Utilize Gemini AI's brainstorming features to generate creative ideas, explore different angles, and overcome writer's block.
- **Content Generation:** Jumpstart your writing process by generating drafts for blog posts, articles, or social media content. Provide Gemini AI with essential details like your target audience, desired tone, and a brief topic description, and let it craft a draft to get you started.

- **Content Repurposing and Expansion:** Breathe new life into existing content! Rewrite sentences or paragraphs for improved clarity, summarize lengthy articles, or expand on existing ideas to generate fresh variations for different platforms.

Tailoring Content to Specific Platforms

While the core message might remain similar, the way you present your content should differ depending on the platform. Gemini AI can assist you in:

- **Blog Post Optimization:** Generate compelling blog post intros, outlines, and even complete drafts tailored to your target audience and blog's overall style.
- **Social Media Magic:** Craft engaging social media captions and posts that resonate with your followers on each platform. Gemini AI can generate catchy headlines, attention-grabbing hooks, and content formats specifically designed for platforms like Twitter, Instagram, or Facebook.

Pro Tip: Experiment with different Gemini AI features for each stage of the content creation process. Combine brainstorming, content generation, and repurposing functionalities to maximize your workflow efficiency.

The following sections will provide step-by-step guides and practical examples to illustrate how to leverage Gemini AI for content creation on various platforms: Blog posts, Articles, and Social Media. Get ready to hit publish with confidence and establish yourself as a consistent content creator!

5.2 Email Marketing and Newsletters: Craft Compelling Messages with Efficiency

In today's digital age, email marketing remains a powerful tool for communication and engagement. This section explores how Gemini AI can streamline your email marketing workflow and empower you to craft compelling messages that resonate with your audience.

Boosting Efficiency: Automating Repetitive Tasks

Save valuable time and free yourself from tedious tasks by leveraging Gemini AI's automation functionalities:

- **Personalized Email Drafts at Scale:** Craft personalized email drafts for your subscribers with ease. Provide Gemini AI with general templates and subscriber data points (e.g., names, purchase history). It can then personalize greetings, product recommendations, or special offer details for each recipient.

- **Data Entry Automation:** Eliminate the tedium of manual data entry when managing your email marketing lists. Utilize Gemini AI to automate tasks like adding new subscribers, segmenting lists based on specific criteria, or updating contact information.

- **Campaign Management Made Easy:** Streamline your email marketing campaigns by automating repetitive tasks like scheduling emails, sending follow-up messages, and generating reports on campaign performance.

Content Creation Powerhouse: Crafting Captivating Email Copy

Gemini AI empowers you to write high-quality email content efficiently:

- **Subject Line Magic:** Craft captivating subject lines that entice recipients to open your emails. Utilize Gemini AI to generate attention-grabbing headlines that clearly communicate the value proposition of your email.

- **Compelling Email Body Copy:** Generate persuasive email body copy that resonates with your target audience. Provide Gemini AI with information about your offer, target audience, and desired tone, and let it craft compelling email content to drive engagement.

Personalization for Enhanced Engagement

Personalization is key to successful email marketing. Gemini AI allows you to:

- **Segment Your Audience:** Create targeted email campaigns by segmenting your subscriber list based on demographics, interests, or purchase history. Gemini AI can assist you in identifying relevant segments and personalizing the content accordingly.

- **Dynamic Content Insertion:** Personalize your emails with dynamic content that changes based on the recipient. This could include greetings by name, product recommendations based on past purchases, or special offers relevant to their interests.

Pro Tip: A/B test different subject lines and email copy variations generated by Gemini AI to see what resonates best with your audience and optimize your email marketing campaigns for maximum impact.

The following sections will provide step-by-step guides and practical examples to illustrate how to leverage Gemini AI for various email marketing tasks, such as crafting compelling subject lines, generating personalized email copy, and automating email campaign workflows. Get ready to transform your email marketing efforts and connect with your audience on a deeper level!

5.3 Advertising Copy and Sales Pitches: Generate High-Converting Content with Gemini AI

Craft persuasive advertising copy and captivating sales pitches that drive conversions with the help of Gemini AI. This section equips you with the knowledge and tools to leverage AI-powered content generation for maximum marketing impact.

From Awareness to Action: The Power of Compelling Ad Copy

In the competitive world of advertising, grabbing attention and sparking interest is crucial. Gemini AI empowers you to:

- **Brainstorm Winning Headlines:** Craft scroll-stopping headlines that capture attention and entice viewers to learn more about your product or service. Utilize Gemini AI's brainstorming features to generate creative headlines that effectively communicate your value proposition.

- **Compelling Ad Copywriting:** Generate persuasive ad copy that highlights the key benefits of your offering and compels viewers to take action. Provide Gemini AI with details about your target audience, product features, and desired call to action, and let it craft compelling ad copy that resonates with your ideal customer.

- **A/B Testing Made Easy:** Generate multiple variations of ad copy and headlines to test with your target audience. Gemini AI can assist you in creating different creative concepts to identify the versions that perform best and optimize your ad campaigns for maximum return on investment (ROI).

The Art of Persuasion: Crafting High-Converting Sales Pitches

The goal of a sales pitch is to convince potential customers that your product or service is the perfect solution to their needs. Gemini AI can be your secret weapon for crafting winning sales pitches:

- **Understanding Your Audience:** Develop buyer personas to understand your target customer's pain points, desires, and motivations. Gemini AI can assist you in analyzing customer data and market research to create buyer personas that inform your sales pitch strategy.

- **Tailored Pitches that Convert:** Craft personalized sales pitches that resonate with each customer's unique needs. Provide Gemini AI with information about the specific customer or prospect, and it can help you generate targeted messaging that highlights the most relevant benefits and addresses their potential concerns.

- **Overcoming Objections with Confidence:** Be prepared to address common customer objections. Utilize Gemini AI to brainstorm persuasive counter-arguments and craft responses that effectively overcome objections and move the sale forward.

Pro Tip: Don't rely solely on AI-generated content. Use Gemini AI's suggestions as a starting point, and personalize the copy with your own unique voice and brand storytelling to create truly impactful marketing materials.

The following sections will provide step-by-step guides and practical examples to illustrate how to leverage Gemini AI for various advertising and sales copywriting tasks. Get ready to craft compelling ad copy, tailor sales pitches to specific audiences, and close more deals with the help of AI!

Chapter 6: Unlocking the Power of AI for Research and Information Gathering

Welcome, knowledge seekers! This chapter dives into the exciting world of AI-powered research assistance. Gemini AI empowers you to gather information efficiently, analyze complex data, and gain deeper insights to inform your research endeavors.

From Tedious Tasks to Efficient Exploration: Streamlining the Research Process

Research can be a time-consuming process. Gemini AI helps you:

- **Effortless Information Gathering:** Gather relevant information from various sources with ease. Simply provide keywords or topics, and Gemini AI can search online articles, academic journals, databases, and other web resources to compile the data you need.

- **Intelligent Content Curation:** Go beyond simple data collection. Gemini AI can analyze the gathered information, identify key themes and trends, and curate relevant content that aligns with your research focus.

- **Citation Management Made Easy:** Keep track of your research sources effortlessly. Utilize Gemini AI's citation management features to organize references, generate bibliographies in various formats, and avoid plagiarism concerns.

AI-Powered Analysis: Extracting Meaning from Data

Data is powerful, but extracting meaningful insights can be challenging. Gemini AI empowers you to:

- **Text Analysis and Summarization:** Analyze large volumes of text and generate concise summaries that highlight the most important information. This allows you to quickly grasp the key points of complex research papers or lengthy articles.

- **Data Visualization Tools:** Transform complex data sets into visually compelling charts and graphs. Gemini AI can generate various data visualizations that make it easier to identify trends, patterns, and relationships within your data.

- **Comparative Analysis:** Compare and contrast information from different sources. Gemini AI can help you identify similarities and differences between research findings or arguments presented in various articles or studies.

Building a Strong Research Foundation: Credibility and Fact-Checking

Verifying the credibility of information is crucial for any research project. Gemini AI can assist you in:

- **Source Evaluation:** Assess the credibility and trustworthiness of online sources. Gemini AI can analyze factors such as website authority, author expertise, and publication date to help you identify reliable sources of information.
- **Fact-Checking on Autopilot:** Ensure the accuracy of your information by leveraging Gemini AI's fact-checking capabilities. Access credible sources and verify the validity of data to maintain the integrity of your research findings.

- **Avoiding Plagiarism:** Gemini AI can help you steer clear of plagiarism by properly citing sources and ensuring your writing reflects your own analysis and interpretation of the data.

The Art of Effective Research Queries: Crafting Powerful Prompts

The quality of your research results heavily depends on the prompts you provide to Gemini AI. Here are some tips for crafting effective queries:

- **Specificity is Key:** Provide clear and specific keywords or topics that accurately reflect your research focus. The more specific your query, the more relevant information Gemini AI can gather.
- **Context Matters:** Provide context to your query whenever possible. This could include details about the research field, methodology, or desired outcomes to guide Gemini AI in the right direction.

- **Refine and Iterate:** Don't be afraid to refine your queries based on the initial results. As you delve deeper into your research, adjust your keywords or prompts to explore specific aspects in more detail.

Pro Tip: Combine different Gemini AI functionalities throughout your research process. Utilize information gathering, analysis tools, and fact-checking features to build a comprehensive understanding of your research topic.

The following sections will provide step-by-step guides and practical examples to illustrate how to leverage Gemini AI for various research tasks. Get ready to transform your research approach, become a more efficient information gatherer, and gain deeper insights to fuel your projects!

6.1 Research Made Easy: Curating Information, Summarizing Articles, and Fact-Checking

Welcome, fellow scholars! This section dives into how Gemini AI can streamline your research workflow and empower you to gather information efficiently, synthesize complex ideas, and ensure the accuracy of your findings.

Effortless Information Gathering: Let Gemini AI Be Your Research Assistant

Gone are the days of spending hours sifting through endless search results. Gemini AI can be your personal research assistant, helping you:

- **Identify Relevant Sources:** Provide keywords or a broad research topic, and Gemini AI will scour the web to find relevant articles, academic journals, and other web resources.

- **Curated Content Delivery:** Move beyond overwhelming search results pages. Gemini AI can analyze the gathered information, identify the most pertinent sources, and curate a collection of high-quality content directly aligned with your research focus.

- **Advanced Search Capabilities:** Refine your search and delve deeper into specific aspects of your topic. Utilize Gemini AI's advanced search filters to narrow down results by publication date, author expertise, or specific website domains to ensure you find the most credible and relevant information.

Pro Tip: When providing keywords or a research topic to Gemini AI, consider incorporating Boolean operators like "AND," "OR," and "NOT" to create more precise search queries. This will help Gemini AI identify information that directly intersects with your specific research needs.

Transforming Complexity into Clarity: Summarization Powerhouse

Research often involves encountering lengthy articles or complex academic papers. Gemini AI can be your secret weapon for efficient information processing:

- **Concise Summaries:** Generate summaries that capture the key points of research papers or lengthy articles. This allows you to quickly grasp the main arguments, methodologies, and findings without getting bogged down in intricate details.
- **Customizable Summarization Levels:** Control the level of detail in your summaries. Choose between brief bullet points highlighting the main takeaways or opt for more comprehensive summaries that provide a deeper understanding of the content.

- **Targeted Summaries:** Focus on specific sections of an article or research paper. Instruct Gemini AI to summarize particular sections, such as the introduction, methodology, or conclusion, to pinpoint the information most relevant to your research inquiry.

Building Trust in Your Research: Ensuring Accuracy and Avoiding Plagiarism

Verifying the credibility of information is paramount for academic integrity. Here's how Gemini AI can assist you:

- **Source Evaluation and Fact-Checking:** Don't rely solely on the first search result. Gemini AI can analyze the credibility of online sources by considering factors like website authority, author expertise, and publication date. It can also help you fact-check information by cross-referencing it with reliable sources.

- **Citation Management Made Easy:** Keep track of your research sources and avoid plagiarism concerns. Utilize Gemini AI's citation management features to organize references, automatically generate bibliographies in various academic formatting styles, and ensure proper attribution of information in your research projects.

- **Maintaining Originality:** While summaries and paraphrasing can be helpful research tools, it's crucial to maintain originality in your writing. Use Gemini AI-generated summaries as a springboard to develop your own interpretations and arguments, ensuring your research reflects your unique analysis and insights.

The following sections will provide step-by-step instructions and practical examples to illustrate how to leverage Gemini AI for information gathering, article summarization, and fact-checking throughout your research journey. Get ready to become a more efficient researcher and build a strong foundation for your academic endeavors!

6.2 Competitive Analysis: Leverage AI to Gain Insights into Your Market

Welcome, market mavericks! This section explores how Gemini AI can empower you to conduct intelligent competitor analysis, gather valuable market insights, and develop winning strategies to stay ahead of the curve.

Unveiling the Competitive Landscape: Identifying and Researching Competitors

Understanding your competitors is crucial for business success. Gemini AI can assist you in:

- **Competitor Identification:** Go beyond your most obvious rivals. Utilize Gemini AI's market research capabilities to identify both direct and indirect competitors who might be vying for the same customer base.
- **In-Depth Competitor Analysis:** Research your competitors comprehensively. Gather information about their products or services, target audience, marketing strategies, brand reputation, and online presence, all within the Gemini AI platform.

- **Competitive Benchmarking:** Benchmark your own performance against your competitors. Analyze their strengths and weaknesses, identify potential gaps in your offerings, and use these insights to inform your product development and marketing strategies.

Pro Tip: When conducting competitor analysis with Gemini AI, leverage its information gathering features to collect data from various sources. This could include company websites, social media profiles, customer reviews, and industry publications.

Extracting Knowledge from Data: Analyzing Market Trends and Customer Insights

Raw data is powerful, but turning it into actionable insights requires analysis. Gemini AI empowers you to:

- **Market Trend Analysis:** Identify emerging market trends and customer preferences. Utilize Gemini AI's data analysis tools to uncover patterns and shifts in consumer behavior to inform your product development and marketing strategies.

- **Social Listening Made Easy:** Gain valuable insights from social media conversations. Use Gemini AI to monitor brand mentions, analyze customer sentiment towards your competitors, and identify potential areas for improvement in your own brand messaging.
- **Survey Analysis on Autopilot:** Effortlessly analyze customer survey data. Gemini AI can summarize key findings, identify recurring themes, and generate reports to help you understand your target audience better and tailor your offerings accordingly.

AI-Powered Strategy Development: Formulating Winning Moves

The ultimate goal of competitor analysis is to develop effective business strategies. Here's how Gemini AI can assist you:

- **Strategic Planning Assistant:** Utilize Gemini AI's brainstorming features to generate creative ideas for new product development, marketing campaigns, and market positioning strategies.

- **Data-Driven Decision Making:** Don't base your decisions on guesswork. Leverage the market insights gleaned from Gemini AI to make data-driven choices that give you a competitive edge.
- **Scenario Planning and Risk Assessment:** Use Gemini AI to explore different market scenarios and assess potential risks associated with your business decisions. This allows you to develop contingency plans and mitigate potential challenges proactively.

The following sections will provide step-by-step guides and practical examples to illustrate how to leverage Gemini AI for various competitor analysis tasks. Get ready to transform your approach to market research, gain a deeper understanding of your competitive landscape, and develop winning strategies to dominate your market!

6.3 Staying Ahead of the Curve: Utilizing AI for Trend Discovery and Future Planning

Welcome, future-focused thinkers! In today's rapidly evolving world, the ability to anticipate trends is crucial for success. This section explores how Gemini AI can empower you to become a trend hunter, identify emerging patterns, and leverage those insights for future planning in various domains.

Demystifying the Future: Spotting Emerging Trends with AI

The future might seem uncertain, but with the help of AI, you can gain a glimpse into what's on the horizon. Here's how Gemini AI can assist you in trend discovery:

- **Data-Driven Trend Analysis:** Analyze vast amounts of data from various sources, including social media conversations, news articles, and industry reports. Gemini AI can identify emerging patterns, predict future trends, and highlight potential opportunities before they become mainstream.

- **Weak Signal Detection:** Go beyond the obvious trends. Gemini AI can uncover subtle shifts in data that might be overlooked by traditional methods, allowing you to identify niche trends with high growth potential.

- **Scenario Planning for Different Futures:** Explore various possibilities using Gemini AI's scenario planning features. Model different future outcomes based on potential trends and assess their impact on your business, industry, or area of interest.

Pro Tip: When using Gemini AI for trend discovery, focus on identifying trends that align with your specific field or area of expertise. This will allow you to gain more actionable insights and tailor your future planning accordingly.

From Insights to Action: Utilizing Trends for Strategic Planning

Foresight is only valuable if you translate it into action. Here's how Gemini AI can assist you in leveraging trend insights for future planning:

- **Strategic Roadmaps for the Future:** Develop comprehensive strategic roadmaps based on anticipated trends. Utilize Gemini AI to brainstorm potential actions, assess risks and opportunities, and create a clear path forward to navigate the evolving landscape.

- **Innovation and Opportunity Identification:** Identify opportunities for innovation inspired by emerging trends. Gemini AI can help you explore new product or service ideas, develop creative marketing strategies, and position yourself at the forefront of change.

- **Risk Management and Mitigation:** Proactively address potential challenges posed by future trends. Utilize Gemini AI's scenario planning features to identify potential risks and develop contingency plans to mitigate their impact on your projects or endeavors.

The following sections will provide step-by-step guides and practical examples to illustrate how to leverage Gemini AI for various trend discovery and future planning tasks. Get ready to transform your approach to the future, develop a proactive mindset, and seize the opportunities presented by emerging trends!

Chapter 7: Beyond the Basics: Advanced Techniques for Supercharged Productivity

Welcome, productivity champions! Having mastered the core functionalities of Gemini AI, this chapter delves into advanced techniques to maximize your efficiency and transform yourself into a productivity powerhouse.

The Art of Automation Mastery: Crafting Complex Workflows

We've explored automating repetitive tasks, but what about building intricate workflows? Here's how to leverage Gemini AI's automation features for advanced use cases:

- **Multi-Step Workflow Creation:** Connect multiple Gemini AI features to create complex workflows. Imagine automatically generating a social media post based on a summarized news article or crafting an email draft incorporating data points from your CRM.
- **Conditional Logic for Intelligent Automation:** Incorporate conditional logic into your workflows. Instruct Gemini AI to perform different actions based on specific criteria, making your automations more intelligent and adaptable.

- **Trigger-Based Automation:** Set up automated tasks triggered by specific events. For example, automatically generate a blog post outline whenever you publish a new article on a different platform.

Pro Tip: Break down complex tasks into smaller, actionable steps. This will make it easier to map them onto Gemini AI's workflow automation features and ensure your automations function smoothly.

Data Powerhouse: Leveraging Gemini AI for Data Analysis and Visualization

Gemini AI goes beyond content creation. It can be your data analysis companion:

- **Data Cleaning and Preprocessing:** Clean and prepare your data for analysis. Utilize Gemini AI's data cleaning features to address inconsistencies, missing values, or formatting errors to ensure the accuracy of your analysis.
- **Data Analysis and Insights Generation:** Extract meaningful insights from your data. Gemini AI can analyze data sets, identify trends and patterns, and generate reports or data visualizations to communicate your findings effectively.

- **Data Visualization Made Simple:** Transform complex data into visually compelling charts and graphs. Gemini AI offers various data visualization options to make your data easier to understand and interpret for yourself or your audience.

Pro Tip: When presenting data insights, leverage Gemini AI's content generation features to craft compelling narratives that effectively communicate your findings and their significance to the recipient.

Collaboration Reimagined: Streamlining Teamwork with Gemini AI

Boost your team's productivity with Gemini AI's collaboration features:

- **Centralized Knowledge Hub:** Consolidate all your team's essential information within Gemini AI's platform. Store documents, meeting notes, brainstorming ideas, and project plans in a central location accessible to all team members.

- **Real-Time Task Management:** Assign tasks, track progress, and collaborate on projects seamlessly within Gemini AI. Utilize features like task delegation, progress updates, and file sharing to keep your team aligned and accountable.

- **AI-Powered Brainstorming:** Generate creative ideas together using Gemini AI's brainstorming functionalities. This can be particularly helpful for remote teams to overcome geographical barriers and foster collaborative innovation.

The following sections will provide step-by-step instructions and practical examples to illustrate how to leverage Gemini AI for advanced automation, data analysis, and collaborative teamwork scenarios. Get ready to unlock your full potential and accomplish more in less time!

7.1 Building Custom Workflows: Automating Repetitive Tasks with Gemini AI

Welcome back, automation enthusiasts! This section dives into the exciting world of custom workflow creation using Gemini AI. By chaining together different functionalities, you can automate complex sequences of tasks and free up valuable time to focus on higher-level projects.

From Simple to Complex: Understanding Workflow Components

- **Actions:** These are the specific tasks that Gemini AI will perform within your workflow. Actions can include generating content (text formats, emails, social media posts), data analysis, information gathering from web sources, and more.
- **Triggers:** These are the events that initiate the workflow. Triggers can be manual (e.g., clicking a button) or automatic (e.g., receiving a new email).

- **Conditions:** (Optional) These are specific criteria that determine how the workflow progresses. You can use conditional logic to create more intelligent automations that adapt to different situations.

Building Your First Workflow: A Step-by-Step Guide

Let's walk through an example of building a custom workflow to automatically generate social media posts based on new blog articles:

1. **Identify the Trigger:** The trigger for this workflow will be the publication of a new blog post on your website.

2. **Define the Actions:** The first action will be to instruct Gemini AI to access your website and identify the latest blog post. The second action will be to generate a social media post summarizing the key points of the article. You can specify the target social media platform (e.g., Twitter, Facebook) and desired post format (e.g., short blurb with a link to the full article).

3. **Refine and Test:** Once you've defined the trigger and actions, test your workflow thoroughly to ensure it functions as expected. Publish a test blog post and observe if Gemini AI automatically generates the corresponding social media post.

Pro Tip: Start with simple workflows and gradually increase complexity as you gain experience. Break down complex tasks into smaller, more manageable steps to ensure your workflows run smoothly.

Conditional Logic: Adding Intelligence to Your Workflows

Conditional logic allows you to create more sophisticated workflows that adapt to different scenarios. Here's an example:

- You can set up a condition to check the length of the blog post summary generated by Gemini AI. If the summary exceeds the character limit for the target social media platform, you can instruct Gemini AI to automatically shorten it further.

Exploring Advanced Workflow Applications

The possibilities for custom workflow creation are vast. Here are a few additional ideas:

- Automatically generate email responses based on specific email content.
- Compile data from various sources and generate reports with data visualizations.
- Monitor social media mentions and generate alerts based on relevant keywords.

The following sections will provide more practical examples and in-depth explanations to equip you with the knowledge and skills to build advanced workflows that streamline your work and boost your productivity across various tasks and projects.

7.2 Integrating with Other Tools: Expanding Your AI Ecosystem

Welcome back, productivity champions! Gemini AI is a powerful tool, but its true potential unfolds when integrated with your existing workflow and the other applications you rely on daily. This section explores how to leverage Gemini AI's integration capabilities to create a seamless AI ecosystem that supercharges your efficiency.

Breaking Down Data Silos: Connecting Gemini AI to Your Favorite Apps

Many popular applications offer integration options through APIs (Application Programming Interfaces). By establishing connections between Gemini AI and these tools, you can:

- **Automate Data Flow:** Seamlessly exchange data between Gemini AI and other applications. Imagine automatically populating a CRM system with lead information captured from a website form or generating reports in another tool based on data analyzed by Gemini AI.

- **Streamlined Workflows:** Craft even more intricate workflows that span across different applications. Combine Gemini AI's functionalities with features from other tools to automate complex processes and eliminate the need for manual data entry or repetitive tasks across platforms.
- **Enhanced Functionality:** Expand the capabilities of both Gemini AI and your other tools. Integrations can unlock new functionalities or streamline existing processes, allowing you to achieve more with less effort.

Exploring Popular Integration Options

Here are some examples of how Gemini AI can integrate with popular tools to enhance your workflow:

- **Calendar Apps:** Automatically schedule meetings or add tasks to your calendar based on information extracted from emails or documents.
- **CRM Systems:** Enrich your CRM with data from website forms, social media interactions, or automatically generate personalized email outreach based on customer information.

- **Project Management Tools:** Streamline project management by automatically generating reports based on project data or creating tasks within your project management tool based on information from emails or discussions.

Pro Tip: Identify the applications you use most frequently and explore their integration options. Many project management tools, CRM systems, and even calendar apps offer functionalities to connect with external tools like Gemini AI.

Beyond Pre-Built Integrations: Utilizing Zapier for Advanced Automation

If your desired integration isn't readily available, fret not! Platforms like Zapier allow you to create custom integrations between Gemini AI and virtually any application. This unlocks a whole new world of possibilities for crafting highly customized workflows that perfectly suit your specific needs.

The following sections will provide step-by-step instructions and practical examples to illustrate how to leverage popular integration options and explore using Zapier to create custom integrations. Get ready to transform your workflow by connecting Gemini AI with the tools you already use and love, creating a powerful AI ecosystem that fuels your productivity!

7.3 Advanced Customization: Tailoring Gemini AI to Your Specific Needs

Welcome, fellow alchemists! Having explored Gemini AI's core functionalities and delved into advanced techniques, this section empowers you to truly personalize your AI experience. By understanding Gemini AI's customization options, you can tailor it to your unique workflow and maximize its effectiveness for your specific tasks and goals.

Understanding User Preferences: Personalization for Optimal Performance

Gemini AI offers various features that allow you to personalize your experience:

- **Content Style and Tone:** Instruct Gemini AI on your preferred writing style and tone. Do you need formal and professional writing for business documents, or a more casual and conversational tone for social media content? Guiding Gemini AI with these preferences will ensure the generated content aligns with your needs.

- **Domain-Specific Language:** Train Gemini AI to understand your specific industry jargon or terminology. Provide it with relevant glossaries, technical documents, or examples of your desired writing style within your field to enhance the accuracy and relevance of the generated content.

- **Data Preferences and Integration:** Connect Gemini AI with the applications you use most frequently and specify your preferred data flow. This ensures seamless information exchange and avoids data silos that can hinder workflow efficiency.

Pro Tip: Don't be afraid to experiment with different customization options. As you use Gemini AI more and provide it with feedback, it will learn your preferences and adapt to your specific needs over time.

Customizing Workflows for Maximum Efficiency

We've explored building custom workflows, but you can further personalize them:

- **Saved Workflows and Templates:** Save frequently used workflows as templates for quick access and reuse. This allows you to automate repetitive tasks with a single click and streamlines your workflow considerably.

- **Customizable Triggers and Actions:** While Gemini AI offers a variety of built-in triggers and actions for workflow creation, some functionalities might allow for customization. Explore the options to tailor triggers and actions to perfectly match your specific needs.

- **Feedback and Refinement:** Continuously monitor and refine your workflows. Pay attention to the outputs generated by Gemini AI and provide feedback to improve its accuracy and effectiveness over time.

The Art of Effective Prompts: Mastering Communication with Gemini AI

The quality of your prompts significantly impacts the quality of Gemini AI's outputs. Here are some tips for crafting effective prompts:

- **Clarity and Specificity:** Provide clear and specific instructions. The more precise your prompts, the better Gemini AI will understand your request and generate content that aligns with your expectations.
- **Context is Key:** Don't just provide keywords. Offer additional context about your goals, target audience, or desired tone to guide Gemini AI in the right direction.

- **Examples and References:** If possible, include examples or reference materials that showcase your desired style or format. This provides valuable insights for Gemini AI to interpret your prompts more accurately.

Pro Tip: Think of yourself as a conductor guiding an orchestra. With clear and well-defined prompts, you can instruct Gemini AI to deliver the content and functionalities that perfectly suit your needs.

The following sections will provide step-by-step instructions and practical examples to illustrate how to leverage customization options, refine workflows, and craft effective prompts to transform Gemini AI into a truly personalized assistant that empowers you to achieve more, faster.

Chapter 8: The Ethical Use of AI: Responsible Practices for a Brighter Future

Artificial intelligence (AI) holds immense potential to revolutionize various aspects of our lives. However, alongside its benefits, ethical considerations regarding AI development and use are paramount. This chapter explores key principles for responsible AI practices to ensure AI empowers a brighter future for all.

Transparency and Explainability: Demystifying AI Decisions

- **Algorithmic Transparency:** Strive to understand how AI systems arrive at their decisions. This empowers users to assess the logic behind AI-generated outputs and builds trust in the technology.

- **Explainable AI (XAI):** Utilize XAI techniques to make AI decision-making processes more transparent. This allows users to comprehend the reasoning behind AI outputs and identify potential biases.

Avoiding Bias: Mitigating Algorithmic Prejudice

- **Inclusive Training Data:** Ensure the data used to train AI models is diverse and representative of the population it will serve. Biased training data can lead to discriminatory AI outputs.

- **Bias Detection and Mitigation:** Continuously monitor AI systems for potential biases and implement strategies to mitigate them. Techniques like fairness audits and bias detection algorithms can help identify and address bias in AI models.

Human Oversight and Control: Maintaining Human-in-the-Loop AI

- **Human oversight:** AI systems should not operate in a vacuum. Implement human oversight mechanisms to ensure AI functionality aligns with ethical principles and human values.
- **Human-Centered Design:** Prioritize human well-being in AI development and use. Focus on creating AI systems that augment human capabilities and complement human decision-making.

Privacy and Security: Protecting User Data

- **Data Privacy Principles:** Adhere to data privacy regulations and best practices. Ensure user data is collected, stored, and used ethically and transparently.
- **Data Security Measures:** Implement robust data security measures to protect user data from unauthorized access, misuse, or breaches.

Accountability and Responsibility:

- **Clear Ownership and Accountability:** Establish clear ownership and accountability for AI systems. Determine who is responsible for the development, deployment, and potential negative impacts of AI.
- **Algorithmic Impact Assessments:** Conduct algorithmic impact assessments to evaluate the potential social and ethical implications of AI systems before deployment.

The Future of AI: A Collaborative Effort

The ethical development and use of AI is a shared responsibility. Here's how we can work together:

- **Open Dialogue and Collaboration:** Foster open dialogue and collaboration among stakeholders, including developers, policymakers, ethicists, and the public, to establish ethical frameworks for AI development and use.

- **Continuous Learning and Improvement:** The field of AI is constantly evolving. Commit to ongoing learning and improvement in AI ethics to address emerging challenges and ensure responsible AI practices remain at the forefront.

By embracing these principles and working collaboratively, we can harness the power of AI for good and build a future where AI empowers positive change and benefits all of humanity.

8.1 Understanding AI Bias: How to Mitigate Bias in Gemini AI Outputs

AI, like any tool, can reflect the biases present in the data it's trained on. This section dives into how bias can manifest in Gemini AI outputs and equips you with strategies to mitigate its influence.

Understanding Bias: Types and How They Affect AI

Bias can creep into AI systems in various ways:

- **Data Bias:** Training data that reflects societal biases can lead AI models to perpetuate those biases in their outputs. For example, if an AI is trained on a dataset containing mostly male CEOs, it might generate content that reinforces gender stereotypes in leadership positions.

- **Algorithmic Bias:** The algorithms used to develop AI models might inherently contain biases. For instance, an algorithm designed to identify patterns in loan applications might favor applicants from certain demographics based on historical data.

Impact of Bias in Gemini AI Outputs

Bias in Gemini AI outputs can manifest in several ways:

- **Unequal or Inaccurate Content Generation:** Gemini AI might generate content that favors certain viewpoints or demographics over others. This can be problematic for tasks like generating summaries of news articles or creating marketing copy.

- **Unintended Stereotypes:** Biased outputs might reinforce stereotypes or perpetuate discriminatory practices. For example, Gemini AI might generate descriptions of professions that rely on outdated gender roles.

Mitigating Bias in Gemini AI: A Multi-Pronged Approach

There's no single solution to eliminate bias entirely, but a multi-pronged approach can significantly reduce its influence:

- **Critical Evaluation of Prompts:** Carefully consider the potential for bias in your prompts. Avoid using language that could steer Gemini AI towards biased outputs. For example, instead of prompting for a "strong leader," you could prompt for a "decisive and articulate leader."

- **Data Diversity is Key:** Whenever possible, provide Gemini AI with access to diverse datasets that represent a variety of viewpoints and demographics. This helps to reduce the influence of bias in the training data.
- **Fact-Checking and Verification:** Don't rely solely on Gemini AI outputs. Critically evaluate the generated content and fact-check information to ensure accuracy and mitigate potential bias.

- **Feedback and Refinement:** Provide feedback to Gemini AI when you identify biased outputs. Over time, with user feedback, Gemini AI can learn to generate more balanced and unbiased content.

Pro Tip: Stay informed about advancements in AI fairness research. As the field evolves, new techniques and tools will emerge to help mitigate bias in AI systems like Gemini AI.

Remember: Ethical AI use starts with us, the users. By being mindful of potential biases and implementing these mitigation strategies, we can ensure that Gemini AI empowers us to create inclusive and informative content.

The following sections will provide specific examples and guidance on how to craft prompts that minimize bias, identify biased outputs, and leverage feedback mechanisms to improve the fairness and accuracy of Gemini AI's results.

8.2 Transparency and Attribution: Maintaining Ownership and Crediting AI Assistance

As AI continues to integrate into our lives, understanding transparency and attribution becomes crucial. This section explores why it's important to be transparent about using AI tools like Gemini AI and how to properly credit its contributions to your work.

Why Transparency Matters: Building Trust and Avoiding Misrepresentation

Transparency about using AI tools like Gemini AI benefits both users and audiences:

- **Building Trust:** Openly acknowledging AI assistance builds trust with your audience. It demonstrates your commitment to ethical practices and allows them to evaluate the information presented with a comprehensive understanding of its creation process.
- **Avoiding Misrepresentation:** Attributing AI-generated content appropriately ensures you don't take credit for work produced by AI. This fosters intellectual honesty and avoids plagiarism concerns.

Transparency in Action: Disclosing AI Use in Different Scenarios

Here's how to be transparent about using Gemini AI in various situations:

- **Academic Research and Writing:** Clearly disclose that you used Gemini AI to summarize research papers or generate citations. Mention it in the methodology section of your paper and provide proper attribution in your bibliography.

- **Content Creation:** If you leverage Gemini AI to generate content for blog posts, social media captions, or marketing materials, disclose its use. You can do this with a simple footnote or parenthetical statement within the content itself.
- **Data Analysis and Reporting:** Be transparent about using Gemini AI to analyze data or generate reports. Acknowledge its role in the process while taking ownership of the interpretation and insights derived from the data.

Finding the Right Balance: Crediting AI While Highlighting Your Expertise

Striking a balance between acknowledging AI's contribution and showcasing your own expertise is key:

- **Focus on Human-AI Collaboration:** Frame AI use as a collaborative effort. You provide the prompts, curate the information, and exercise your judgment to ensure the final output aligns with your goals.

- **Highlight Your Expertise:** The critical thinking, analysis, and creative direction you provide are essential. Focus on how you leverage your expertise to shape the outputs from Gemini AI into valuable content or insights.

Transparency Best Practices: Clear and Consistent Communication

Here are some tips for clear and consistent communication about AI use:

- **Simple and Direct Language:** Avoid overly technical jargon when explaining AI use. Strive for clear and concise language that your audience can understand.
- **Focus on the Benefits:** Explain how using AI enhances your work or improves the final product. Highlight the efficiency, creativity, or additional insights gained through AI collaboration.

The following sections will provide practical examples of how to disclose AI use in various contexts, including academic writing, content creation, and data analysis. You'll also find guidance on crafting clear and concise language to communicate your AI collaboration effectively.

8.3 The Future of AI and Work: Preparing for an AI-Powered Workforce

The future of work is rapidly evolving, and artificial intelligence (AI) is poised to play a transformative role. This section explores how AI will likely impact the workplace and equips you with strategies to prepare for a successful career in an AI-powered workforce.

The Rise of Human-AI Collaboration: A New Era of Work

AI is not here to replace human workers; rather, it will augment human capabilities and redefine how we work. Imagine AI handling repetitive tasks, freeing up human time for creative problem-solving, strategic thinking, and tasks that require emotional intelligence and social skills – areas where humans will continue to excel.

The Evolving Workplace: New Skills and Opportunities

The rise of AI will necessitate the development of new skillsets:

- **Digital Literacy and AI Fluency:** An understanding of AI capabilities and limitations will be essential. Workers will need to be comfortable working alongside AI tools and leverage their functionalities effectively.
- **Critical Thinking and Problem-Solving:** As AI handles routine tasks, human roles will shift towards higher-order thinking skills. The ability to analyze complex situations, solve non-standard problems, and make sound decisions will be paramount.

- **Adaptability and Continuous Learning:** The pace of technological change will continue to accelerate. Developing a growth mindset and embracing lifelong learning will be crucial for navigating the evolving workplace landscape.

Preparing for the Future of Work: Actionable Strategies

Here's how you can prepare yourself for an AI-powered future:

- **Identify Your Transferable Skills:** Analyze your existing skillset and identify transferable skills that will remain valuable in an AI-driven workplace. Communication, collaboration, creativity, and critical thinking are strong assets to cultivate.
- **Embrace Continuous Learning:** Seek out opportunities to learn about AI and its potential applications in your field. Online courses, workshops, and industry publications can be valuable resources.

- **Develop Your Human-Centered Skillset:** Focus on honing skills where human expertise shines. Refine your communication, leadership, and interpersonal skills to position yourself for success in a collaborative human-AI work environment.
- **Network and Stay Informed:** Connect with professionals in your field and stay updated on emerging trends in AI and its impact on your industry.

The Future of Work is a Shared Journey

The transformation of the workplace with AI is a collaborative effort. Here's what different stakeholders can do:

- **Educational Institutions:** Integrate AI literacy and relevant skill development into curriculums to prepare future generations for the AI-powered workforce.
- **Businesses and Organizations:** Invest in reskilling and upskilling initiatives to equip employees with the necessary skills to thrive in an AI-driven work environment.

- **Policymakers:** Develop policies that promote responsible AI development and ensure a smooth transition for workers as AI integration evolves in the workplace.

By embracing continuous learning, developing a human-centered skillset, and fostering collaboration between various stakeholders, we can navigate the future of work with optimism and ensure a successful transition to an AI-powered workforce that benefits all.

Chapter 9: The Competitive Edge: Leveraging Gemini AI for Business Success

Welcome, business mavericks! In this chapter, we delve into the strategic application of Gemini AI to propel your business to new heights. By harnessing its capabilities across various aspects of your operations, you can gain a competitive edge in today's dynamic market landscape.

9.1 Boosting Marketing and Sales Strategies: AI-Powered Solutions for Growth

Welcome, marketing and sales warriors! In today's competitive landscape, creativity, data-driven decision-making, and efficient use of time are crucial for success. This section explores how Gemini AI can empower you to supercharge your marketing and sales efforts, generate high-quality leads, and convert them into loyal customers.

From Scattered Efforts to Strategic Campaigns: AI-Driven Marketing and Sales

Gone are the days of isolated marketing and sales initiatives. Gemini AI fosters a holistic approach, analyzing data to inform targeted marketing campaigns that drive qualified leads directly into your sales funnel.

Marketing with Gemini AI: Targeted Outreach and Content Creation

- **Content Marketing Powerhouse:** Beat writer's block and generate compelling content to fuel your marketing campaigns. Utilize Gemini AI to craft blog posts, social media captions, email newsletters, and even white papers on industry-relevant topics tailored to your target audience.

- **Targeted Audience Identification:** Don't waste time with generic marketing blasts. Gemini AI can analyze market data and customer demographics to identify your ideal customer profile, allowing you to focus your marketing efforts on the audiences most likely to convert.

- **Personalized Marketing Campaigns:** Craft personalized marketing messages that resonate with your audience. Gemini AI can generate personalized email content, segment your customer base for targeted outreach, and recommend content tailored to individual customer interests.

Pro Tip: Integrate Gemini AI with your marketing automation platform to seamlessly personalize email campaigns, automate lead nurturing sequences, and track campaign performance for continuous improvement.

Sales Enablement with Gemini AI: Qualifying Leads and Boosting Conversions

- **Lead Scoring and Qualification:** Not all leads are created equal. Utilize Gemini AI to analyze customer data and interactions, assign scores to leads based on their potential value, and prioritize your sales outreach efforts towards the most qualified leads.

- **Sales Pitching and Proposal Generation:** Craft persuasive sales pitches and tailored proposals that resonate with your leads. Utilize Gemini AI to highlight key selling points aligned with your target customer's needs and generate data-driven proposals that convince them to convert.

- **Objection Handling and Negotiation Support:** Equip your sales team with effective objection handling strategies. Gemini AI can analyze historical sales data to identify common customer objections and generate counter-arguments to help your sales team overcome challenges and close deals.

Pro Tip: Train your Gemini AI to understand your unique sales methodology and communication style. This ensures generated content aligns with your approach and resonates with your target audience.

The following sections will provide step-by-step instructions and practical examples to illustrate how to leverage Gemini AI for content marketing, targeted outreach, lead qualification, and crafting persuasive sales pitches. Get ready to unleash the power of AI to transform your marketing and sales funnel and achieve sustainable business growth!

9.2 Optimizing Internal Processes: Streamlining Operations with AI Assistance

Welcome, champions of efficiency! Every minute counts in today's fast-paced business environment. This section dives into how Gemini AI can optimize internal processes across various departments within your organization, freeing up valuable time and resources for your team to focus on strategic initiatives.

From Manual Mayhem to Automated Magic: AI-Powered Workflow Transformation

Repetitive tasks, data overload, and communication bottlenecks can hinder operational efficiency. Gemini AI automates workflows, analyzes data to generate insights, and facilitates seamless communication, transforming the way your business operates.

Supercharge Your Departments with Gemini AI

- **Human Resources:** Streamline recruiting processes by using Gemini AI to screen resumes, schedule interviews, and generate interview questions. Utilize its data analysis capabilities to identify top talent and improve retention strategies.
- **Finance and Accounting:** Automate data entry tasks, generate financial reports, and conduct fraud detection analysis with Gemini AI. Its data processing capabilities can save significant time and ensure accuracy in financial operations.

- **Customer Service:** Provide 24/7 customer support with AI-powered chatbots powered by Gemini AI. These chatbots can answer frequently asked questions, troubleshoot common issues, and route complex requests to human agents, resulting in improved customer satisfaction.

Pro Tip: Identify repetitive tasks within each department that are well-suited for automation using Gemini AI. Focus on high-volume, rule-based processes to maximize efficiency gains.

Data-Driven Decision Making: Leveraging Gemini AI for Strategic Insights

- **Data Analysis and Reporting:** Turn raw data into actionable insights with Gemini AI. Utilize its capabilities to analyze sales data, customer feedback, and market trends, empowering data-driven decision-making across all levels of your organization.

- **Sales Forecasting and Pipeline Management:** Improve sales forecasting accuracy with Gemini AI's data analysis tools. Identify potential roadblocks in your sales pipeline and proactively address them to optimize sales performance.
- **Project Management and Resource Allocation:** Gain real-time project insights with Gemini AI. Track project progress, identify resource bottlenecks, and optimize resource allocation to ensure projects stay on track and within budget.

Pro Tip: Integrate Gemini AI with your existing business intelligence (BI) tools to consolidate data from various sources, generate comprehensive reports, and gain a holistic view of your organization's performance.

The following sections will provide step-by-step instructions and practical examples to illustrate how to automate tasks within specific departments, generate data-driven reports, and improve decision-making processes across your entire organization. Get ready to unlock the hidden potential within your workflows and propel your business towards operational excellence!

9.3 Staying Ahead of the Innovation Curve: Using AI to Future-Proof Your Business

Welcome, innovation trailblazers! In today's rapidly evolving business landscape, creativity, adaptability, and a willingness to embrace change are essential for survival. This section explores how Gemini AI can fuel your innovation engine, empowering you to identify new opportunities, develop cutting-edge products and services, and stay ahead of the competition.

From Incremental Change to Disruptive Innovation: The Power of AI-Fueled Creativity

Gemini AI augments human creativity by generating new ideas, analyzing vast amounts of information to identify emerging trends, and helping you explore possibilities beyond the traditional brainstorming methods.

Spark Innovation with Gemini AI

- **Brainstorming and Idea Generation:** Jumpstart your innovation sessions with Gemini AI's brainstorming features. Utilize it to explore different design concepts, identify potential solutions to challenges, and generate new product ideas that differentiate you from the competition.

- **Competitive Analysis on Autopilot:** Stay one step ahead of the curve. Utilize Gemini AI to conduct in-depth competitor research, analyze market trends, and identify disruptive technologies that could impact your industry.
- **Data-Driven Product Development:** Develop innovative products and services that resonate with your target audience. Utilize Gemini AI to analyze customer feedback, identify unmet needs, and inform product development roadmaps based on data-driven insights and future market forecasts.

Pro Tip: Cultivate a culture of experimentation within your organization. Encourage your team to use Gemini AI to explore unconventional ideas and challenge existing assumptions to spark truly groundbreaking innovation.

Building a Culture of Continuous Learning: The Key to Long-Term Success

The pace of technological change is relentless. By embracing a growth mindset and continuously learning about new advancements in AI and its potential applications, you can ensure your business remains future-proofed in the ever-evolving market landscape.

Here are some tips to foster a culture of continuous learning within your organization:

- **Invest in AI training and workshops:** Equip your team with the knowledge and skills to leverage Gemini AI effectively.

- **Encourage exploration and experimentation:** Provide opportunities for your team to explore the various functionalities of Gemini AI and discover new ways to integrate it into their workflows.
- **Stay up-to-date on AI trends:** Organize knowledge-sharing sessions to discuss the latest advancements in AI and its potential impact on your industry.

By combining the power of Gemini AI with a culture of continuous learning and a commitment to innovation, you can transform your business into a thriving force in the dynamic world of tomorrow!

The following sections will provide step-by-step instructions and practical examples to illustrate how to leverage Gemini AI for brainstorming sessions, competitive analysis, data-driven product development, and fostering a culture of continuous learning within your organization. Get ready to unleash your innovative potential and chart a course for sustainable business growth in the face of ongoing technological disruption!

Chapter 10: The Road Ahead: Exploring the Future Possibilities of Gemini AI

Welcome, intrepid explorers of the future! Throughout this guide, you've delved into the impressive capabilities of Gemini AI and witnessed its potential to transform various aspects of your work and personal life. As we conclude this journey, let's explore the exciting possibilities that lie ahead for Gemini AI and speculate on how it might continue to shape our world in the years to come.

10.1 Emerging Trends in AI: What to Expect from Gemini AI in the Coming Years

The field of Artificial Intelligence (AI) is rapidly evolving, and Gemini AI is poised to stay at the forefront of these advancements. Here's a glimpse into some exciting trends that could shape the future of Gemini AI in the coming years:

Enhanced Reasoning and Learning:

- **Going Beyond Pattern Recognition:** Current AI excels at pattern recognition, but future iterations like Gemini AI might develop causal reasoning capabilities. This would allow it to understand cause-and-effect relationships and draw more nuanced conclusions from data.

- **Continuous Learning and Improvement:** Imagine Gemini AI continuously learning from user interactions and data exposure. This could enable it to adapt its responses, refine its understanding of the world, and provide more personalized and insightful results over time.

Understanding and Responding to Emotions:

- **Emotional Intelligence for AI:** As AI technology progresses, Gemini AI might develop the ability to recognize and respond to human emotions. This could revolutionize customer service interactions by enabling AI to provide empathetic support and tailor its communication style based on the user's emotional state.

- **Human-AI Relationship Management:** Gemini AI could become a trusted confidante, understanding and responding to your emotional cues. Imagine using it to brainstorm ideas, work through challenges, or receive supportive feedback in a way that acknowledges your emotional well-being.

Increased Creativity and Problem-Solving:

- **Breaking the Mold: Creative Thinking with AI:** Gemini AI's creative capabilities might flourish, allowing it to generate original ideas that go beyond simple paraphrasing or rearranging existing information. This could spark innovation across various fields and assist with problem-solving in unexpected and ingenious ways.

- **Going Beyond Structured Data:** Current AI often struggles with unstructured data like images, audio, and video. Future versions of Gemini AI might process and understand these data types more effectively, opening doors to new creative applications like generating emotional responses to music or writing poems inspired by works of art.

These are just a few possibilities, and the future holds even more exciting advancements!

By leveraging these emerging trends, Gemini AI could transform the way we work, learn, and interact with the world around us. Imagine a future where AI assists us in creative endeavors, provides emotional support, and solves complex problems in innovative ways. With responsible development and human-centered design principles at the forefront, Gemini AI has the potential to become a powerful tool for positive change in the years to come.

10.2 Unlocking Your Full Potential: Continuous Learning and Exploration

As we wrap up our exploration of Gemini AI, it's crucial to remember that **you** are the key to unlocking its true potential. Gemini AI is a powerful tool, but it thrives on human input, curiosity, and a growth mindset. Here's how continuous learning and exploration can empower you to maximize the benefits of Gemini AI in your life:

Embrace Experimentation:

- **Don't be afraid to step outside your comfort zone** and try new things with Gemini AI. Explore its various features, play around with different prompts, and discover unexpected functionalities that can enhance your workflow.
- **Think outside the box:** Challenge yourself to use Gemini AI in unconventional ways. Can it help you brainstorm business ideas, write song lyrics, or debug a complex problem? The possibilities are endless!

Become a Feedback Champion:

- **Your input shapes the future of Gemini AI.** Provide constructive feedback on your experience. Report any issues you encounter, suggest improvements to existing features, and share ideas for new functionalities.

- **The more you engage with Gemini AI's development team, the better it can adapt to user needs and become a truly valuable tool** for everyone.

Embrace Continuous Learning:

- The field of AI is constantly evolving. Stay curious, seek out new knowledge about AI advancements, and understand its limitations as well as its capabilities.
- This will allow you to better partner with Gemini AI and leverage its potential to its fullest. The more you understand AI, the more creative and strategic you can be in incorporating it into your tasks.

Remember, you are not just a user of Gemini AI; you are a collaborator. By continuously learning, experimenting, and providing feedback, you shape the future of this powerful tool and unlock its potential to empower you in extraordinary ways.

Here are some additional tips to keep the learning journey going:

- **Follow industry publications and blogs** focusing on AI advancements to stay up-to-date on the latest trends.
- **Enroll in online courses or workshops** to deepen your understanding of AI concepts and applications.

- **Connect with other AI enthusiasts online or in person** to share ideas, learn from each other's experiences, and broaden your perspective on the potential of AI.

By embracing continuous learning and exploration, you can ensure that Gemini AI remains not just a handy tool, but a powerful partner on your journey to unlocking your full potential. **The future is full of possibilities, and together with Gemini AI, you can shape it in remarkable ways!**

10.3 Join the Community: Sharing Experiences and Collaborating with Other Early Adopters

Welcome to the forefront of innovation! As an early adopter of Gemini AI, you have the unique opportunity to shape the future of this groundbreaking technology. By sharing your experiences and collaborating with other users, you can collectively unlock its full potential and accelerate its development.

The Power of Community: Why Collaboration Matters

Being part of a community offers several advantages:

- **Shared Learnings and Best Practices:** Connect with other Gemini AI users to exchange tips and tricks, discover new use cases, and learn from each other's successes and challenges. This collective knowledge enriches everyone's experience with Gemini AI.
- **Accelerated Innovation:** By sharing ideas and collaborating on projects, the user community can contribute to the development of new features and functionalities for Gemini AI. Your insights can directly influence the future roadmap of this powerful tool.

- **Mutual Support and Problem-Solving:** Get help and support from fellow users when you encounter challenges with Gemini AI. The community can provide troubleshooting tips, workarounds for specific tasks, and moral encouragement as you explore the vast capabilities of this AI.

How to Get Involved: Finding Your Place in the Gemini AI Community

Here are some ways to connect with other Gemini AI users and become an active member of the community:

- **Online Forums and Discussion Boards:** Look for dedicated online forums or discussion boards hosted by Gemini AI or on independent platforms frequented by AI enthusiasts. These platforms offer a space to ask questions, share experiences, and engage in conversations about Gemini AI's applications and potential.

- **Social Media Groups:** Join social media groups focused on AI or Gemini AI specifically. These groups provide a platform to connect with users from around the world, share your creative outputs generated with Gemini AI, and participate in discussions about the latest advancements in the field.

- **Attend Events and Workshops:** Look for workshops, conferences, or hackathons centered around AI or Gemini AI. These events offer valuable opportunities to network with other users, learn from industry experts, and collaborate on projects that push the boundaries of what's possible with Gemini AI.

By actively participating in the community, you become more than just a user; you become a pioneer. Your contributions shape the future of Gemini AI and empower others to unlock its potential in groundbreaking ways. Together, you can build a vibrant ecosystem of innovation that drives progress in the exciting world of AI!

Here are some additional tips for fostering a collaborative spirit:

- Be open to new ideas and perspectives.
- Share your knowledge and expertise with others.

- Provide constructive feedback and suggestions for improvement.
- Help others overcome challenges and troubleshoot problems.
- Celebrate the successes of your fellow community members.

Embrace the power of collaboration! As you embark on this journey with Gemini AI, remember that the greatest potential is unlocked not just through individual exploration, but through the collective efforts of a passionate and forward-thinking community!

www.ingramcontent.com/pod-product-compliance
Lightning Source LLC
Chambersburg PA
CBHW071238050326
40690CB00011B/2168